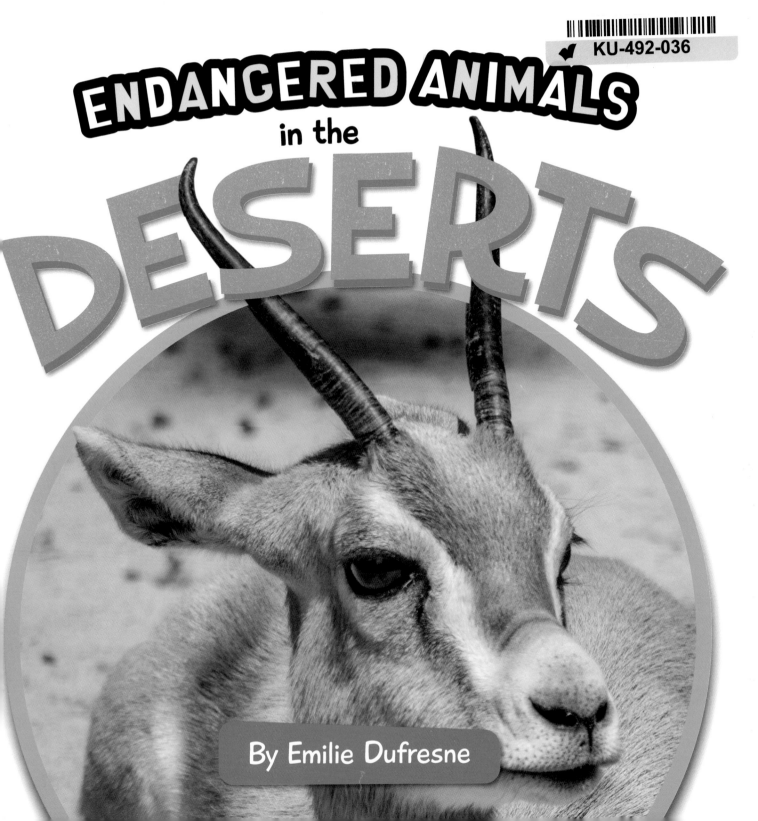

ENDANGERED ANIMALS
in the
DESERTS

By Emilie Dufresne

KU-492-036

BookLife PUBLISHING

©2021
BookLife Publishing Ltd.
King's Lynn
Norfolk PE30 4LS

All rights reserved.
Printed in Malta.

A catalogue record for
this book is available from
the British Library.

ISBN: 978-1-83927-466-4

Written by:
Emilie Dufresne

Edited by:
Madeline Tyler

Designed by:
Jasmine Pointer

All facts, statistics, web addresses and URLs in this book were verified as valid
and accurate at time of writing. No responsibility for any changes to external
websites or references can be accepted by either the author or publisher.

PHOTO CREDITS

All images are courtesy of Shutterstock.com, unless otherwise
specified. With thanks to Getty Images, Thinkstock Photo and
iStockphoto. Cover – Jose Sanchez Munoz. 2–3 – Winston Springwater.
4–5 – Onyx9, idiz, Zebra-Studio. 6–7 – Cathy Withers-Clarke. 8–9
– sunsinger, RethaAretha, KAMONRAT. 10–11 – iliuta goean, Michal
Balada, SlyBrowney, Baly photo. 12–13 – Julian Popov, Mike Mareen,
curiosity, len4ik. 14–15 – Sergei25, OSTILL is Franck Camhi, RudiErnst,
Vectorfair.com. 16–17 – Jason Mintzer, Tim Roberts Photography,
William Radke, U.S. Fish and Wildlife Service / Public domain,
trekandshoot, Park Ji Sun. 18–19 – Wildnerdpix, Sundry Photography,
Wildnerdpix. 20–21 – Mark Marathon / CC BY-SA (https://
creativecommons.org/licenses/by-sa/4.0), PhotoItaliaStudio, msmsha,
S.Borisov. 22–23 – TheOldhiro, Patrick Jennings, Vladeep.

CONTENTS

Words that look like this can be found in the glossary on page 24.

ENDANGERED

When a <u>species</u> of animal is endangered, it means that it is in danger of going extinct. When a species is extinct, it means there are no more of that animal left alive in the world.

Mountain gorillas are an endangered species.

4

There are lots of different reasons that a species might become endangered. If a species' <u>habitat</u> is changed by the <u>climate crisis</u>, it could become endangered.

Many desert animals are facing problems such as drought because of the climate crisis.

CATEGORIES

Different species are put into different categories depending on how <u>threatened</u> they are.

Data Deficient – Not enough information to know what category the species is in

Least Concern – Currently not in danger of going extinct

Near Threatened – Likely to be threatened soon

Vulnerable – Facing a high <u>risk</u> of extinction in the wild

Always check this website to find the most up-to-date information...

www.iucnredlist.org

Endangered – Facing a very high risk of extinction in the wild

Critically Endangered – Facing extremely high risk of extinction in the wild

Extinct in the Wild – When a species can no longer be found in the wild and only lives in <u>captivity</u>

Extinct – When a species no longer exists in the world

DESERT HABITAT

Deserts can either be very hot or very cold places. All deserts get very little rainfall. There are deserts all over the world.

The hot Sahara

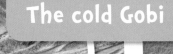

The cold Gobi

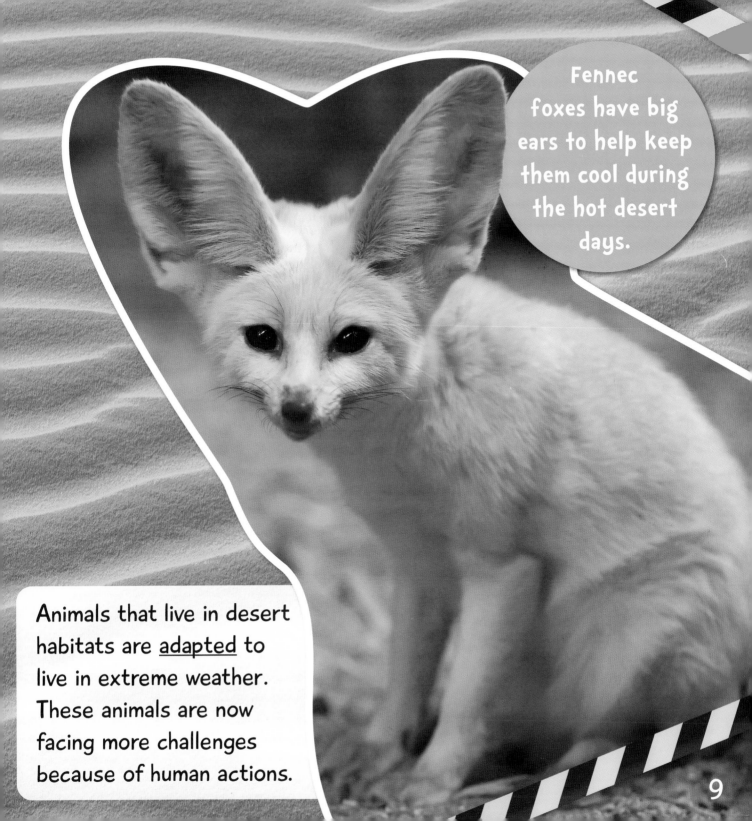

Fennec foxes have big ears to help keep them cool during the hot desert days.

Animals that live in desert habitats are <u>adapted</u> to live in extreme weather. These animals are now facing more challenges because of human actions.

Dorcas

GAZELLES

Droughts make life difficult for dorcas gazelles. Droughts are very long periods with no rain. As deserts are very dry anyway, this means there is even less water and food for animals like the dorcas gazelle.

NAME:
Dorcas gazelle

FOUND:
Across the Sahara

CATEGORY:
Vulnerable

Another problem for dorcas gazelles is the loss of habitat. More and more of their habitat is being used by farmers to look after sheep and goats.

The sheep and goats eat too many plants and don't leave enough for the gazelles.

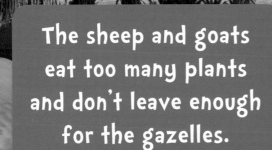

Dorcas gazelles found

ADDAX

For many years, addax were hunted. They move very slowly, which makes them easy for hunters to kill.

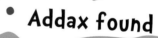
Addax found

The last few wild addax live in a nature reserve. Unfortunately, humans have been using the land on the nature reserve to look for <u>oil</u>.

NAME:
Addax

FOUND:
<u>Nature reserves</u> in the Sahara

CATEGORY:
Critically endangered

POPULATION:
30–90

This can make the addax move away from the protected nature reserves, putting them in danger from hunters.

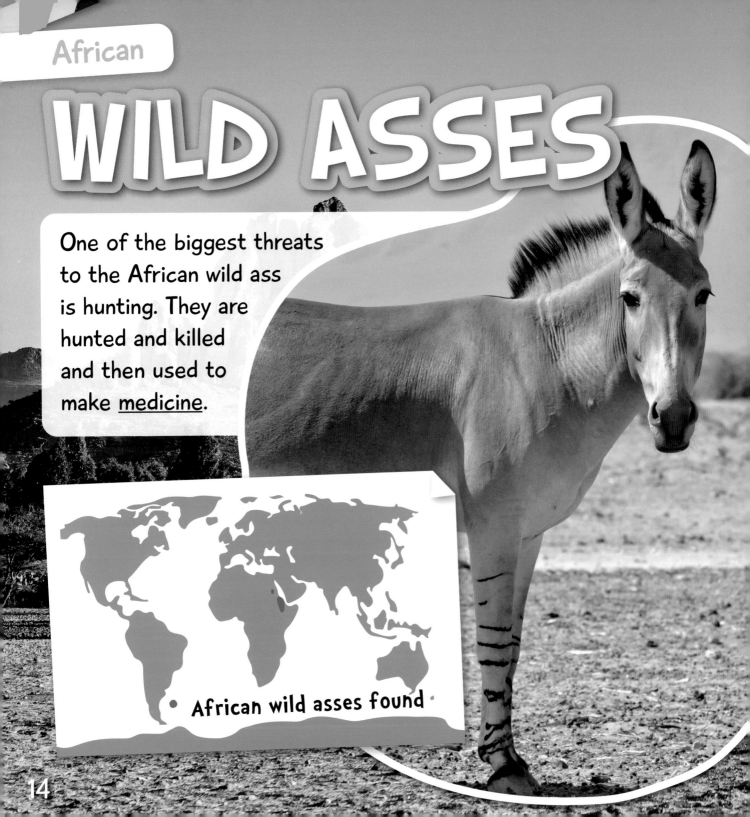

African WILD ASSES

One of the biggest threats to the African wild ass is hunting. They are hunted and killed and then used to make <u>medicine</u>.

African wild asses found

Livestock take the food and drink that African wild asses need for themselves. This can make it difficult for mothers and young wild asses to survive.

NAME:
African wild ass

FOUND:
Eritrea and Ethiopia

CATEGORY:
Critically endangered

POPULATION:
Up to 200

There are projects that try to teach farmers about how to live alongside the asses.

African wild ass calf

Coachella Valley Fringe-Toed
LIZARDS

The Coachella Valley fringe-toed lizard has lost lots of its habitat because of humans building on the land they live on.

NAME:
Coachella Valley fringe-toed lizard

FOUND:
A small area in California, US

CATEGORY:
Endangered

Roads were also built across the lizard's habitat.

Wind blowing sand in Coachella Valley

Coachella Valley fringe-toed lizards found

Humans have also added windbreaks near the lizard's habitat. These stop the wind from blowing sand into the lizard's habitat, but the lizards need this sand to survive.

Desert

PUPFISH

Desert pupfish live in <u>wetlands</u> and marshes in desert areas. They can live in very warm salty water.

However, the water they live in is being moved or used by humans.

NAME:
Desert pupfish

FOUND:
Northwest Mexico and southwest areas of the US

CATEGORY:
Vulnerable

The desert pupfish is also threatened by introduced fish. These are fish which did not live in the same habitat as the desert pupfish at first, but were brought in by humans.

These introduced fish make it hard for the desert pupfish to make young pupfish.

Desert pupfish found

EXTINCT

The desert rat kangaroo is now extinct. People believe that foxes and cats ate so many desert rat kangaroos that the species couldn't survive.

The desert rat kangaroo used to live in Australia.

SUCCESS STORIES

The Mojave desert tortoise is a vulnerable species. Many people work to protect the tortoise by making areas safe for it to live in.

SAVE the ANIMALS!

There are lots of things you can do to help endangered desert species around the world.

EAT LESS MEAT

Farming takes up a lot of land and food that wild animals need. Eating less meat will help them survive.

BE CLEVER FOR THE CLIMATE

Help slow down the climate crisis by turning off lights when you leave a room and putting on a jumper instead of turning on the heating!

GLOSSARY

adapted	when an animal or plant has changed over time to suit where it lives
captivity	kept in a zoo or safari park and not in the wild
climate crisis	the very serious problems that are being caused by human action and the changes these actions make in the natural world
habitat	the natural home in which animals, plants and other living things live
livestock	animals that are kept for farming
medicine	something which is used to make people better when they are ill
nature reserves	areas of land that are protected to keep animals and plants safe
oil	a liquid found underground that flows like water and can be used to power cars and homes
population	the number of animals in a species
risk	when there is a chance that something might happen
species	a group of very similar animals or plants that can create young together
threatened	not sure of whether a type of animal or plant will survive
wetlands	areas of land (usually swamps, marshes or bogs) that are full of water

INDEX